THE SMOKING PUN
CRIMES AGAINST THE LANGUAGE

Thaddeus Taylor

illustrations by Tom Nynas
design by R&D Thinktank
www.randdthinktank.com

Publisher's Cataloging-in-Publication
(Provided by Quality Books, Inc.)

Taylor, Thad.
    The smoking pun : crimes against the language / by
Thad Taylor ; illustrations by Tom Nynas.
    p. cm.
    ISBN 09770469-07

    1. Puns and punning. 2. English language--New words
--Humor. 3. English language--Etymology--Humor.
I. Title.

PN6231.P8T39 2006   818'.607
                               QBI05-600172

First Edition

for
Anonymoose*

*YOU KNOW WHO YOU ARE

INTRODUCTION

If you take a frog apart, carefully, you will not find generic frog insides, plain guts labeled FROG, or tiny tadpoles rowing the master in the general direction of frogness. On the contrary, of course, you will find specialized organs, formed to function in unique ways.

I have found words to be much the same, not full of interchangeable babble-bits, but stuffed and sometimes over-stuffed with dedicated puzzle pieces. Taking them apart has gotten me in trouble. I began to do it unconsciously, often when I was supposed to be paying attention to some other dull thing. Under pressure to multi-task convincingly, I'll admit I put some of them back together incorrectly.

Worse, after the deeds were done, I looked at the original words, which like all words are ragged approximations of thought and feeling, and had no remorse. Maybe I rationalized: at least I hadn't taken a frog apart, and made mistakes in *his* re-assembly.

Most people say no pun intended, or they duck, or they run away. I knew it was no use when people started submitting their puns to me. So, I'm ready to own up to mine, and I want other people to be able to do the same. In the SRS (Stems, Roots, and Seeds) section* you'll find my personal invitation to do just that—but only if you're ready.

—Thad Taylor

* Note the warning from the Surgeon's General. You might decide it's best to just look at the pictures.

DOG WHOSE FOOD IS FANCIER
THAN HIS PEDIGREE

———————————→

FAKE ENTHUSIASM

ANCIENT TYPOGRAPHICAL ERROR

CRUMMY HOST AT A LOUSY RESTAURANT⟶

ONE WHO IS THOROUGHLY
UNQUALIFIED FOR THE JOB ———————————————→

THE DUCK'S BIG SPEECH

SoLILoQUAcK

RELIGIOUS INSULT

———————————————→

OVERWEIGHT MONSTER ⟶

LONG-NECKED DELINQUENT

GIRIFFRAFFE

ONE WHO ANNOYS OTHERS
WITH HIS ALARM CLOCK

⟶

MISSIONARIES FOR SANTA CLAUS ───────────→

SPOOKY CHICKEN

———————————→

HASTILY ASSEMBLED BALLET OUTFIT ⟶

POTATOES

imprompTutu

DEADLY UNDERAGE MARKSMAN ⟶

WhiPperSniper

RELIGIOUSLY AMBIVALENT ⟶

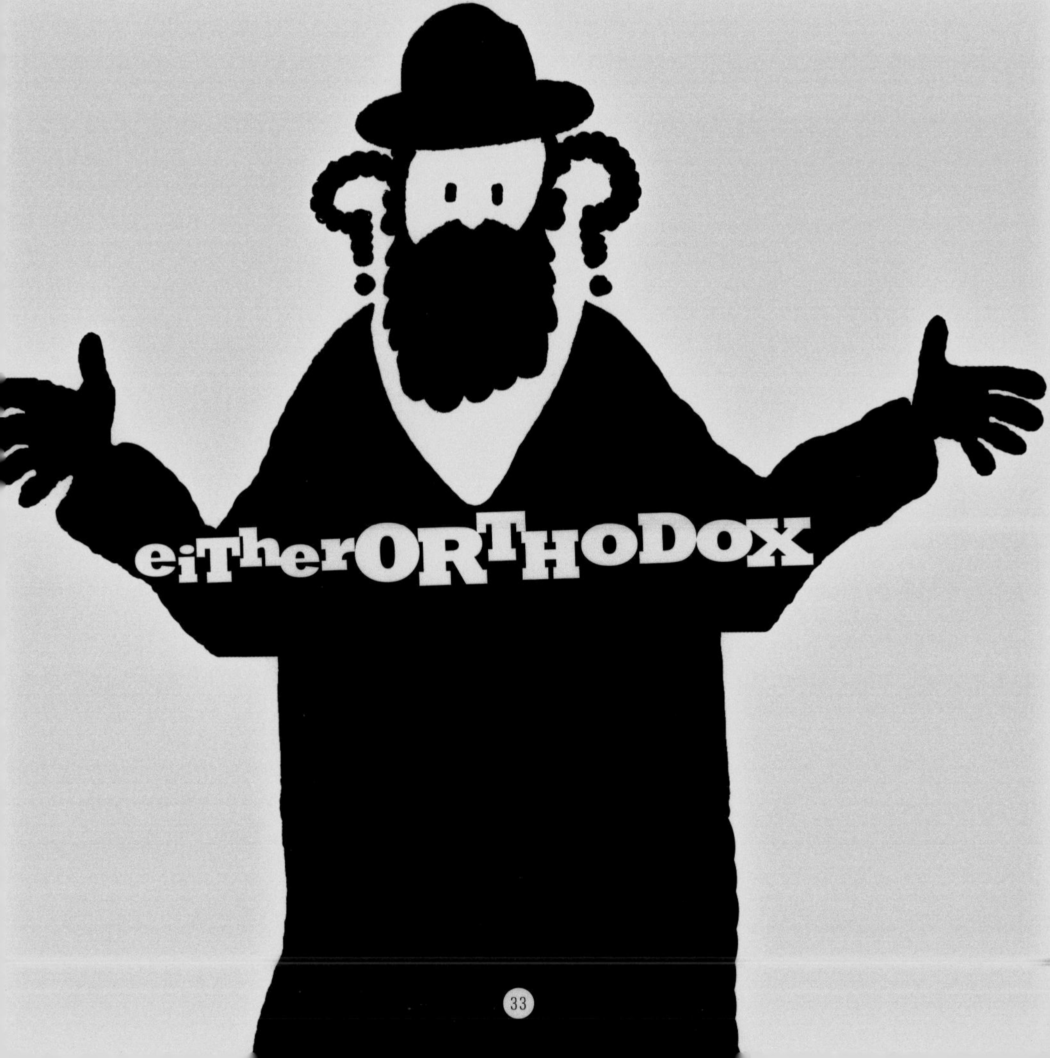
eiTherORTHODOX

WRITTEN ACKNOWLEDGMENT OF
DAMAGE TO A GOLF COURSE

GOD'S ROLLER COASTER $\longrightarrow$

ESPRIT DE CHEERLEADING CORPS   ———————————→

CAMARARARAderie

EXTREME MINIATURE GOLF ⟶

MILD SADNESS

CANDY THAT CAN'T BE COPIED   ⟶

ini**m&mitable**

SHORT POEM BY A CRAZY PERSON

BAND OF THREE PANHANDLERS ⟶

NARCISSIST'S PARADISE

———————→

BROKEN GADGET ⟶

SPAGHETTI TOPPING
FROM LAST NIGHT

DICTATOR'S NEW HAIRDO

———————————→

Coifführer

OFFICE TOTALITARIAN

⟶

EASY CARE TOMB FLOORING

MaUsoLiNOLeUM

BEETHOVEN'S FAVORITE PERFUME

EXTRAORDINARY ACHIEVEMENT
IN EATING

———————→

TOUR DE FORK

LEGAL WORK DONE STRICTLY
FOR ENTERTAINMENT VALUE

EXCELLENT GANGSTER

─────────────────▶

SLAPSTICK GREEK PLAYWRIGHT ⟶

GUILTY PLEA TO CHARGE
OF WASTING PAPER

MEa PulpA

PSYCHIATRIST'S DILAPIDATED DWELLING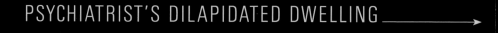

RORSHACK

PSEUDONYM OF OVERWEIGHT AUTHOR

nOm de PLuMp

Sir Mac Beth

BARNYARD WITTICISM

———→

EXTRAMARITAL AFFAIR
BETWEEN TWO KNUCKLEHEADS

SOCIALLY UNACCEPTABLE LAUGHTER $\longrightarrow$

TOILET ROUTINE

COMMODUS OPERANDI

REDNECK DEVIL

———————————————→

BeeLZebuBba

ARCHETYPAL CHILD

———————————→

NATIVE AMERICAN WORD
FOR MISSIONARY

——————————→

EpisCOPalefaCe

STEMS, ROOTS & SEEDS

WARNING: According to the Surgeon's General, questions regarding the true nature of reality may result from even the most casual perusal of this section. Maybe you've got enough on your plate without that. On the other hand, for those with a really high pain threshold, there are literal formulae and loads of helpful extras at www.smokingpun.com.

05 **GOURMUTT:** "pedigree" is from a 15th century Anglo-Norman term *pe de gru* meaning "crane's foot." This seems to have arisen as a result of the common symbol used to illustrate genetic descent, which resembled the foot of a bird.

"Mutt" is short for muttonhead — need a subtler, more meaningful variation on one of our common insults? How about sheep for brains?

"Gourmet" is from the French *grommet* for wine taster, one originally qualified to evaluate the wine merchant's wares, later to provide all kinds of fussy instructions for those who live to eat.

07 **GUNG HOAX:** Victimized term here is originally from Mandarin Chinese for "work together," *honghe*, and became the motto of US Marines in Asia during WW II. This type of enthusiasm is common among investment bankers and CEOs who, despite being bullish on their companies, make ends meet by selling vast chunks of options.

09 **HIEROGLYTCH:** Victim word is from the Greek for "sacred carving" and before spell-checkers pretty much every carving was sacred.

11 **MAITRE D' MINUS:** Been there? Please send your tales of overrated restaurants to www.smokingpun.com. Tales accepted (on the basis of either shimmering wit or cash bribes) will be included in the next hilarious* volume of *THE SMOKING PUN*.

* Would you believe mildly amusing? How about less painful than a herniated disc?

13 **APPLICAN'T**: Having worked in HR for a time, hard to overstate the percentages. You might perform the same elegantly simple operation on a word that means *one whose prayers are never answered*. And those who just pray for work are usually both—applican't and *supplican't*.

15 **SOLILOQUACK**: e.g. "to be a duck or not to be a duck." Victim is from 14th century Latin *solus* "alone" and *loqui* "speak."

17 **METHODIS**: Actually, self-righteous verbal jabs are less likely from a group that repudiated the doctrine of the elect, thanks in large part to the Dutch theologian Jacobus Arminius. He concluded, after much prayer and study, that the whole atonement thing applied to everybody. I reckon some of you, after reading this far, think surely that doesn't include such a one as me, inflicting these kinds of linguistic crimes on the public, but here's my response:

Let him who is without sin cast the first groan.

19 **OBEAST**: Sorry, monsters—this goes with the territory. Svelte is just not nearly as fright-inducing. Sadly, before Monster's gated communities began to be encroached upon by humans, even hideous beasts were for the most part quite fit. Worse still, at the annual conference of Monsters and Nasty Creatures, guidelines were passed overwhelmingly that required all members operating in fitness-obsessed societies to stay at least 20-30 pounds overweight—the better to scare 'em with.

21 **GIRIFFRAFFE**: From the Arabic *zarafa*. Giraffes have a reputation as the nice guys of the jungle, but during their period of enzooment they have gradually become less whole-some. Indeed, zoo observers across the country are reporting a higher incidence of teen smoking among giraffes, especially in zoos where the giraffe compounds are adjacent to the gibbon cages—gibbons, as you may know, are the drug gangs of the zoo kingdom.

Time-out, boys & girls, for FOA
Freedom of Association (It's in the Constitution)

Giraffe, evolved from *Zarafa*, is one of lots of examples of words that we think of as ours, but which were permanently borrowed from other languages. Some purists** frown on this practice, but look at it this way: Before we knew to call it zarafa or some such, most English speakers were spending hyphens at an alarming rate. "Giraffe" was called "long-necked-spotted-thing." That's three hyphens right there. Algebra (also with an Arabic back story) was called "the-whole-let-x-equal-so-and-so-and--let-y-equal-such-and-such-deal." Inevitably, the hyphen commodities market started showing signs of irrational exuberance, and the linguistic powers-that- be (who needed hyphens themselves) authorized wholesale borrowing of foreign words and expressions. And what happened to those who were holding lots of hyphens when the crash occurred? They lost their shirts, some also their pants. But at least they stayed the heck out of the Tulip Mania market of the 1630s, during which, as you undoubtedly know, many ordinary Dutch families were tempted onto the ship of speculation, then torn and tossed and finally thrown against the rocks of financial ruin. By the way, "oopsy daisy" was, for 234 years, "oopsy tulip," referring to this calamity. Then some devious commodities marketers, with worthless inherited tulips still in their portfolios, conspired to bury the truth, using "daisy" just because there was no market for those. The rhyme was purely serendipitous.

** According to <u>The Story of English</u>, one of the essential texts for those who need to know, Bishop Reginald Pecock, during the 16th century, sought to stem the tide of Latinate borrowing, suggesting that we eliminate words like "impenetrable" and instead use hyphen festivals such as "not-to-be-thought-upon-able." Just think how that would have shaken up the punctuation markets!

㉓ BLEEPYHEAD: This subset of the population has increased rapidly since the advent of the snooze alarm. Legislation is pending in several states that would require mandatory penalties for those who: 1) hit the snooze thingee more than twice or

2) are in the shower when the alarm goes off again. I joke about legislation, but this would fall in about the middle of the seriousness continuum in some of our elective assemblies. Go to **www.smokingpun.com** for FREE download of **Shine (the wake-up song)** ©2006 DT Taylor.

25 JEHOHOHOVAH'S WITNESSES: Much taller than Santa's other helpers, more annoying. Try this: keep a copy of either Beowulf or Paradise Lost by your front door, and when the witnesses arrive, proceed onto the front porch and ask, "ever read Beowulf? — just listen to this one little part here, you'll love it." Then simply read aloud at random. Don't desist until they do. In my experience it only takes a stanza or two. Tell your neighbors, each of whom should choose a different lofty masterpiece. Before long, your block will develop a reputation as impregnable (and really well-read).

27 POULTRYGEIST: Thanks to Judge Rucker for this one. Given the opportunity, he would explain that the scary part is what's in those nuggets. *Nugget* apparently is a mid 19th century English regionalism meaning "lump." My guess? "Chicken Lumps" would not have caught on.

29 IMPROMPTUTU: The victim tutu is an alteration of the 17th century French *cucu*, which derives from the Latin *cul* meaning "buttocks." It refers to a dancer's skirt that not only is very short but is made of stiff material, preferably *tulle*, which sticks out from the body. (Trust those nutty French to name a garment after the body part it *fails* to conceal)

31 WHIPPERSNIPER: The victim word derives from *whip snapper*, often a kid on a wagon train or a family vacation, who has nothing to do but crack a whip. Annoying, sure, but right wholesome, in relative terms.

33 EITHERORTHODOX: It's appropriate to hedge my etymological bet on "ambivalent," even though the story seems straightforward: we're fairly certain that it is the German psychologist Eugen Bleuler's fifty-cent coinage, minted by combining the Latin root *ambi* or "both" and the old French *valere*, which means "be strong." So this is not a word that suggests weakness, but a word, especially when used in this context, that suggests the balancing of opposing strengths. Religions that are strong in this way:

a. Don't torture & kill folks* for believing in one God, three gods, seven gods or zero gods.

b. Don't insist that only their sacred book (informed by their unintentionally hilarious exegetical stand-up routines) reveals the Word and Will of God.

c. Don't expel thousands of people from their ancestral homelands, or drag children away from their parents by the hair to baptize 'em.

d. Do recognize the foolishness of certainty, and therefore have more questions than answers.

*Here's a notymological tidbit for ya: *no stone unturned*** is an obfuscating dilution of the expression *no bone unburned*. It refers to the practice of convicting an individual of heresy posthumously, in *extremis* absentia, so to speak, digging up his/her bones and burning them. The advantage of this was only partly spiritual in nature—the bonus was that the dead heretic's estate could then be claimed by the ecclesiastical authorities.

**I know, I know, all you mythology nuts, about the Mardonius/Polycrates/Oracle of Delphi version of the story. But keep it down, would ya? I'm grindin' an ax here—and you now have a delightful instance of *notymology*. Who knows, if you look closely, you may see some more examples in these notes.

Deluxe Feature **no.1**

BONUS CRIMES!

The Cook's Religion ⟶ **Potsandpantheism**

A snack bar at an Israeli punk concert ⟶ **Nosh Pit**

By the way, nosh is a Yiddish word of 20th century provenance, deriving from the Middle High German for "to nibble." The consensus on the victim "mosh" is that it is a corruption of "mash," a sort of stationary stampede of a dance, in some ways resembling the pilgrim scene near Mecca. Please note: consult your doctor before participating in moshes or hajes.

1st Female Muslim Prayer Leader (from Georgia) ──────────> **Ima'am**

If the lightning is gonna strike anyway, let's get it all out of the system now:

Bombastic & heretical Islamic sermon ──────────> **Mullahrkey**
Molester's branch of the Clergy ──────────> **The Rapacy**
Missive from a knuckleheaded pope ──────────> **Imbecyclical**

See how evenhanded? Whaddya expect from a P.K. and a B.S.A.
— no, officer, that's *Preacher's Kid & Back Sliding Agnostic*

35 **AFFIDIVOT:** Victim word is related to medieval Latin *fidere*, which deals with trust—obviously the same root as "fiduciary." Better for your trusted financial advisor to be required to sign one of these than some other kinds of legal documents.

37 **HALLELOOPDELUJAH:** Features a conversion experience between the 3rd hairpin turn and the skyline ascent. Unless you are, of course, SATAN?

39 **CAMARARARADERIE:** Perhaps one of those words that there is little use for. The roots of the victim word, which relates closely to *comrade*, are cited as helping cheerleaders in Communist countries to avoid the vicious infighting that often plagues U.S. squads. But beware of intervening variables: Cheerleader costume manufacture is still nationalized under many totalitarian regimes, which leads to some really unattractively uniform uniforms. Plus, try-outs for Cuban cheerleaders, for example, are under centralized government control, and therefore free of the complications that inevitably result from parental involvement.

41 **LILLIPUTTPUTT**: I for one wish that Jon Swift were alive today. Even though he was, to my way of thinking, needlessly alarmed about the corruption of the English language, he did have a sharp eye for foolishness. You might ask, "But Thad, where would he begin in a world that seems to do such a thorough job of satirizing itself ?" And all I can say (despite my better judgment) is that he could just start small.

43 **MELANBORDERCHOLY**: Victim word comes from the least funny of the four humors, and the condition was early on traced to a scarcity of jokes in the diet, which caused a build-up of dull black bile. "Border" in Border collie refers to the border between England & Scotland, where the breed has been developed for quiet but effective shepherding. Happily, their minimal barking seems to be adaptive for their work with sheep (Babe the pig, you'll recall, had good results with nary a bark) and Border collies seem to be no more susceptible to Seasonal Affective Disorder than other breeds, despite the bloody miserable weather.

45 **INIM&MITABLE**: You might be able to beat the candy cooks, but not the candy lawyers.

47 **HAIKUKU**: Submissions are now being accepted @ **www.smokingpun.com**. Remember the formula: 17 syllables with lines of five seven five. Craziest entry will receive a FREE Cerebral Market T-shirt and have their haikuku published in the next hilarious* volume of *THE SMOKING PUN*. Team submissions will be accepted from "haicrews" but you will have to split the one t-shirt among yourselves.

*See Maxwell Smartish shtick on #11's asterisk.

49 **TRIBUMVERATE**: I don't know about you, but I'm just naturally more generous when I'm walking down the street and *three* guys ask me for money. Etymologically, the *tri* part is obvious, the *vir* is a Latin root for "men." However, instances of three men sharing power or money equally and fairly—even if it's just panhandling proceeds—are as tough to find as Republicans who can do the moonwalk.

51 **METOPIA:** Those of you wondering where to find this on the map, just keep looking in the WATER, like Narcissus hisownself did.

53 **DON'T HICKEY**: Victim is obviously *dohickey*, and the thing itself is indistinguishable, in most cases, from a *whatthehelljamacallit*, a term expressing displeasure with the diminished functionality of said gadget.

55 **RENAISSAUCE**: A quick Public Service Announcement: please, for the sake of the children, Mom & Dad, DATE YOUR LEFTOVERS!

57 **COIFFÜHRER**: From the Latin *cofia* or "helmet" to the French *coife* or "headdress" and the German *führer* or leader. "Hairdo" is classical American.

59 **DESKPOT**: Victim word is from the Greek for "master" and was an honorary title (with no negative connotation) applied to Byzantine rulers. A review of employee handbooks in modern corporations suggests a bewildering range of additional connections to Byzantine life & culture.

61 **MAUSOLINOLEUM:** Victim word #1 derives from the tomb of the 4th century B.C.E King Mausolus, which, while impressive, was in no way EZ Care. Victim #2 is from Latin roots *linum* and *oleum*; the resulting equation is *flax+ oil*.

63 **EAU DE JOY:** Thanks to Beverly Taylor for this one—a product of our high-culture kitchen table. Many people don't realize that, due to his hearing loss, Beethoven developed an extraordinarily acute olfactory capability, making it possible for him to *smell* pitch issues in the second violins, despite the overpowering cologne worn by his concert master.

He recognized the triumph of his 9th Symphony not because of the deafening applause, but, as he later commented, "Smelled pretty good to me."

65 TOUR DE FORK: Only a stickler for technicalities would deny that Takeru Kobayashi is the Lance Armstrong of Professional Competitive Eating. It's true he doesn't use a fork, but this 144 pound eating machine has recently consumed 100 pork buns in 12 minutes, 83 vegetarian dumplings in 8 minutes, *eat cetera*, y'all, and has pioneered methods now being emulated by high school football players everywhere.

67 PRO BOZO: Go to **www.smokingpun.com** for a FREE download of **Right & Wrong (or The World's Funniest Lawyer)** ©2006 DT Taylor.

69 CRÈME DE LA CRIME: In this case, because we are speaking of the underworld, the crème rises to the bottom.

71 EURIPPEDYOUPANTSIDES: I know this does not display the level of E.I. (etymological integrity) that learned readers such as yourselves are entitled to. So sue me. Just please pronounce it as Bill Shakespeare would have when he needed an extra syllable: *you-rip-pid-you-pants-i-dees.*

73 MEA PULPA: Samuel Johnson insulted some of the writers of his day by calling them "paper wasters." Most of their guilty pleas, however, were insincere or part of a literary convention of self-deprecation. Even Bill Shakespeare did it, to wit:

> **How can my Muse want subject to invent**
> **While thou dost breathe, that pour'st into my verse**
> **Thine own sweet argument, too excellent**
> **For every vulgar paper to rehearse?**

As we now know, his recurring argument that her beauty would outlast his material was wrong on its face.

75 RORSHACK: What do you make of this one? Best answer submitted to **www.smokingpun.com** will be included in (God help us) Vol. 2.

77   **NOM DE PLUMP:** A caveat: if one name is used for the author's cookbooks and one for his or her mystery thrillers, use a taster for new recipes.

79   **BON MOO**: Victim is *bon mot*, literally "good word," and is usually used to refer to a witticism that targets someone else. And by the way, it is commonly accepted, since Orwell's <u>1984</u>, that pigs are the smart guys on the farm, but animal husbandry experts, some of whom, strangely enough, are women, have recently been discovering that cows are the comedians, and that they speak a sort of animal Esperanto, with innumerable refinements and inflections on the "moo" sound, enabling them to entertain their fellow animals with everything from Rodney Dangerfield type no-respect jokes to sophisticated riffs and wry commentaries on Hegelian dialectics.

81   **ADOLTERY:** Victim is from the Latin *adulterare*, meaning "to corrupt," so there's nothing etymological that suggests one must be chronologically or psychologically mature to engage in it. If both people are knuckleheaded and married, it would properly be termed "double adoltery." The story of "dolt" is uncertain, but it seems to have been around since the 16th century to refer to someone without intelligence—just in case there was a person like that.

83   **GUFFAUX PAS:** Clearly, a simple though painful collision of the onamatopoeic "guffaw" and the higherfalutin "faux pas." And the best example I can think of for this one comes, alas, from personal experience:

My older brother was a preacher's kid just as I was. We had the same parents and all. Yet, verily, his transgressions were as the sand upon the shore, as the stars in the sky, as all the tiny little particles of stuff that don't seem to be serving any real purpose— indeed, just one damn thing after another. One Sunday, somewhere between the prayer of confession and the anthem, he whispers to me, right there in our near-the-front pew, that a little contest would be fun. "Let's see who can hit the other the *softest*." And, to my eternal shame, I fell for it, going first and, if I do say so myself, hitting him really, really, *really* softly—I mean this has got to be in the running for one of the major league soft hits. Of course, he hauls off and wallops me in the same arm that was predestined to be a bully-magnet in junior high. He then says, "You win!" and proceeds to guffaux pas. Shook the pew, he did. Probably my Dad heard about it from some stuffy choir member, who thought the preacher man would whip us good. But we were fortunate— the God my Dad believes in has a pretty good sense of humor.

85 COMMODUS OPERANDI: Before DNA testing, a surprising number of criminals were traced by canny detectives using subtle patterns in the way crooks performed their toilet. Indeed, modus was an abbreviation of *commodus* used by Scotland Yard gumshoes, attempting to protect the delicate sensibilities of the Victorian public. *Gumshoe* dates from 1906 and referred either to the rubber-soled footwear of detectives, or to the "gum" that got stuck on their shoes in all those bathrooms.

87 BEELZEBUBBA: Here I go joshing with my good friend Bubba—see, it's all those trucks in my Bright Red state that make me: **A** Sensitive to bubbasticity **B** A very defensive driver.

89 JUNGSTER: That'd be the one to clone.

91 EPISCOPALEFACE: There were lots of other Native American words for missionary in the literature. But this was the only one suitable for a family publication.

Deluxe Feature **no.3**

BONUS DEFINITIONS!

matching words@**www.smokingpun.com**

Solo canoodling?

A Floridian's bureaucratic ordeal?
(thanks to Peter Koelling)

A sanctuary for critics?

Doctrinal Q&A with Martin Luther?
(thanks to Tom Zawadzki)

Assorted leftovers?

Cash for glowing blurb?
(hint: see back cover)

The page-turning thumb lick?

A measurement of one's conservative tendencies?

A Personal Invitation

As promised in the introduction, I invite you to inflict your linguistic crimes on the world, too! Here's a handy form, a quick & easy way to say, "Hey, Thad, I got one for ya."

G.O.F.Y. FORM

Definition: _____

Word: _____

Name of contributor: _____

AKA (or purely fabricated name): _____

(We understand if you want to remain anonymous)

E-Mail Address: _____

T-Shirt Size: S   M   L   XL

FREE Cerebral Market T-Shirt for submissions selected for publication*

MILK CARTON SECTION

Definition missing a word: _____

Word missing a definition: _____

* Selections are the sole responsibility of Thad & his bad-tempered drinking buddies.

ACKNOWLEDGMENTS

I guess I should start by thanking God, who thus far has not chosen to smite me. I'd also like to thank the Founding Fathers for including Freedom of Association in the Constitution. I thank my wife & partner Beverly for honoring the "for worse" deal in our vows and my daughter Juliet for understanding that I might have to wear a silly disguise soon. And because of the nature of this book, some may view the remaining acknowledgments as closely akin to blame-shifting, but it would not be true to say that these people didn't help me, often at considerable risk to their careers and/or reputations:

Dr. James Ivy, for patiently kicking my punctuational butt, and **Peter Koelling**; both of these guys have been ready to laugh when I needed them to, even if it meant getting slugged by their wives. **Ed Conroy**, who saw more there than met the eye, and helped me to substantiate it. **Charlie Athanas**, whose extraordinary work you can sample at www.burningcity.com. **Rod Mills**, a light in the retail darkness. **Bill Von Behren & Trip Worden**, for very informative lunches. **Wes Ulmer**@www.sd-tech.net, for more computer wizardry than I deserve. **Tom & Lila Walker**, who proved to me that not all garage sales are worthless. **Tom Zawadzki**, contributor/kindred spirit, and the Quarry friends. **My Mom & my Dad**, whom I've agreed not to name, **my brother Ben & my sister Marla**, who continue to acknowledge *me*. Most especially, I'd like to thank **Tom Nynas**, for allowing the book to become a labor of his love, too. And more than most especially, I thank my other brother, **Doug Rucker**, and his wonderfully creative company, **R&D Thinktank**.

CRIMES OF MY OWN

CRIMES OF MY OWN

CRIMES OF MY OWN